Welcome to the wonderful world of clarinet playing. Your teacher has shown you how to hold your instrument and make a sound on the mouthpiece.

Let's play our first song!

1. Our First Note

NEW NOTE "E"

2. Our Second Note

NEW NOTE "F"

3. Three's a Crowd

4. Four In a Row

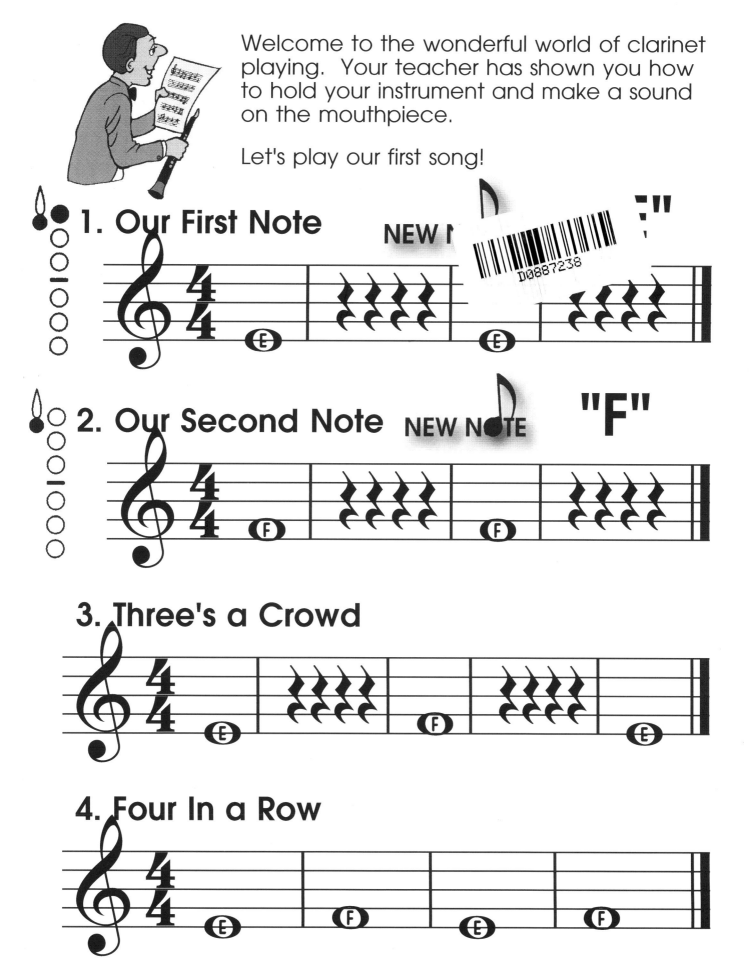

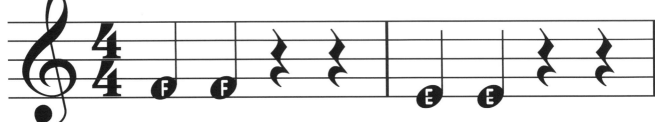

Quarter notes get one beat of sound.

Whole notes get four beats of sound.

5. A Funny Pair

Quarter note rests get one beat of silence.

6. Skate Board Sam

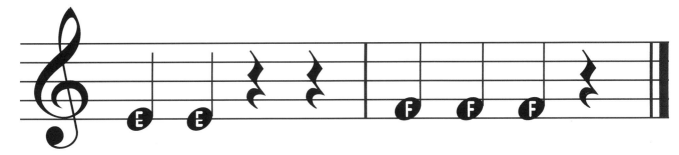

7. Catch That Note

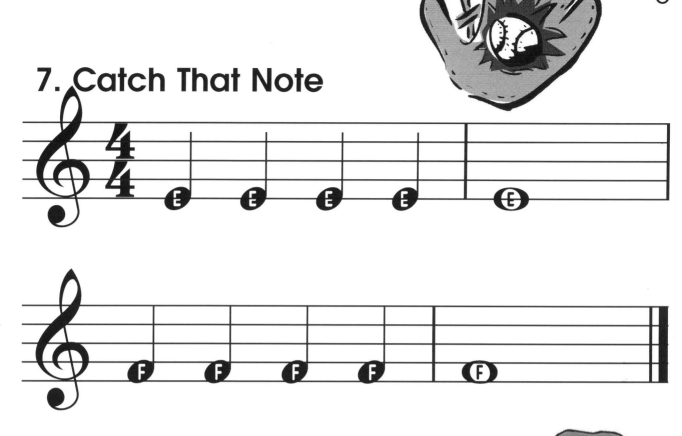

8. Keep On Blowin'

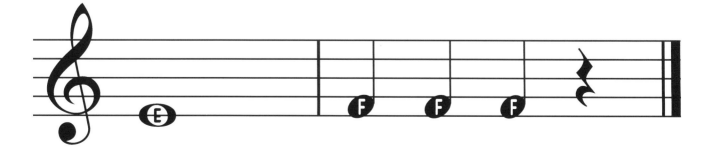

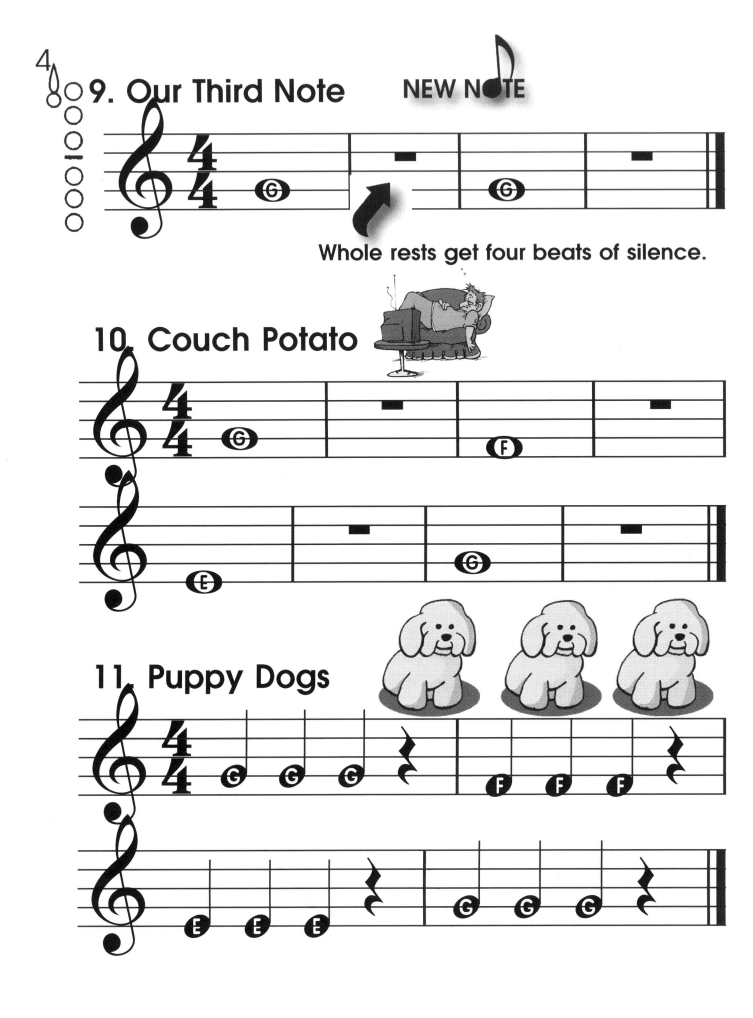

12. Our Fourth Note

NEW NOTE

13. Apple for the Teacher

6

14. Our Fifth Note

NEW NOTE

15. Bumper Cars

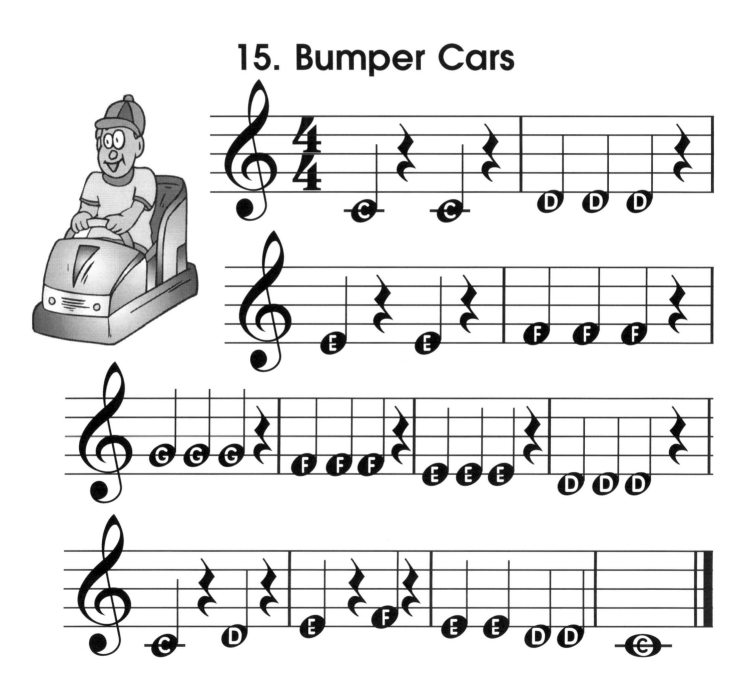

Half Note

Two Beats of Sound

16. Half Notes Happen

17. Hot Cross Buns

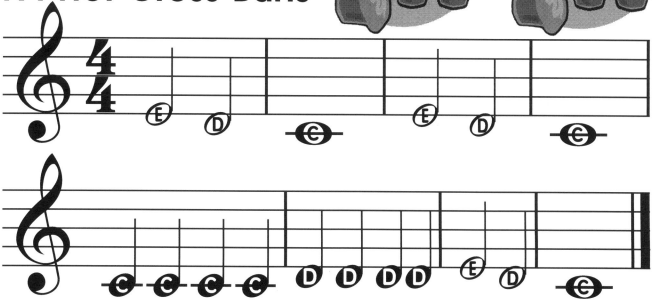

8 Notes are written on
lines and spaces called
the "staff".

How many lines can you find?

How many spaces can you find?

18. High Dive

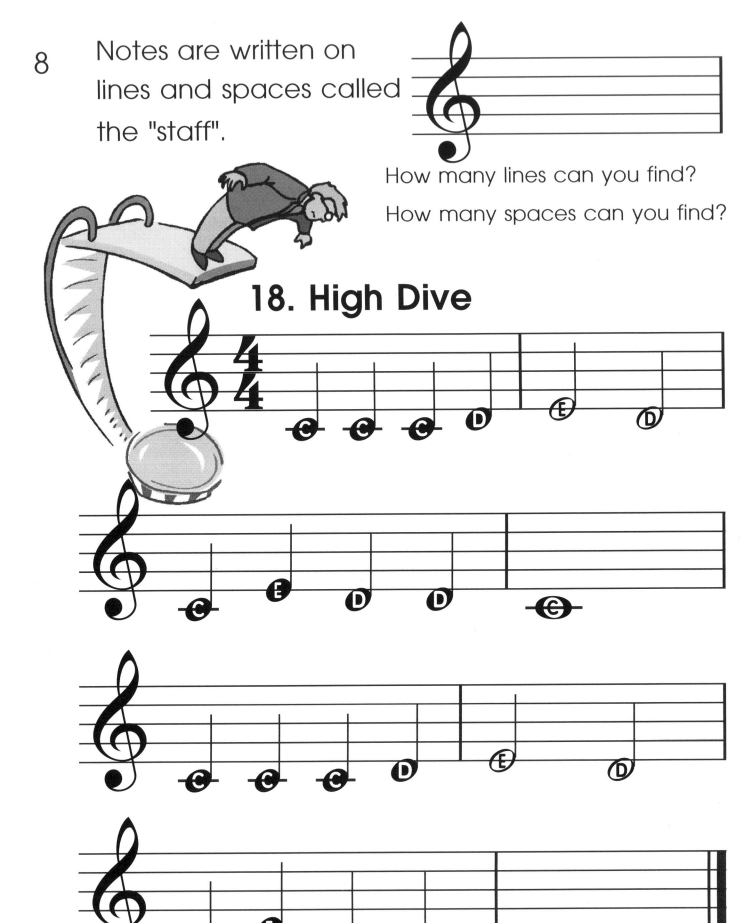

19. Mary Had a Little Lamb

www.bandfunbook.com

20. Bad News Bears

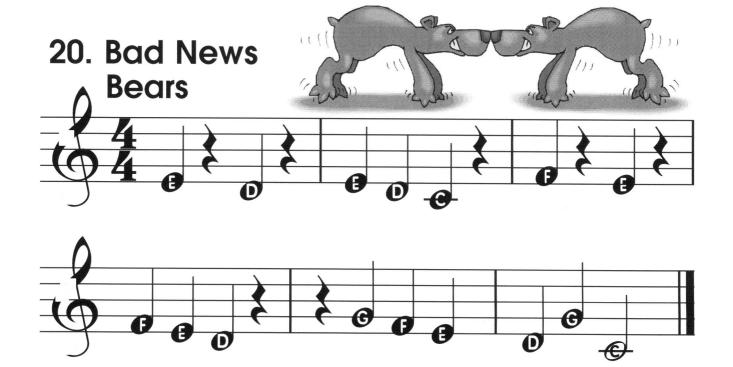

10

21. Dreydl, Dreydl

22. Notes Without Letters

NEW NOTE

23. Shoo Fly, Don't Bother Me!

24. Crazy Tonguing

Rhythm Fun

Eighth Notes One eighth note gets 1/2 count. Two eighth notes get ONE count.

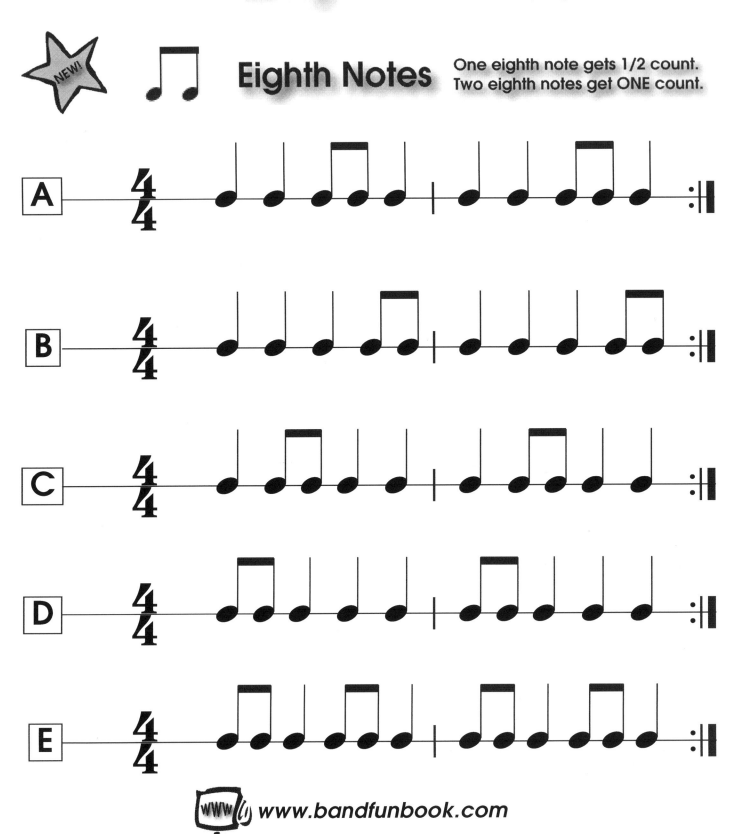

www.bandfunbook.com

25. Yankee Doodle Cha Cha

26. Caribbean Cruise

27. Country Hoe Down

13

28. Eighth Note Slide

Repeat Sign

NEW!

A double bar with TWO DOTS at the end of the measure tells you to REPEAT the music.

29. The Cabbage Song

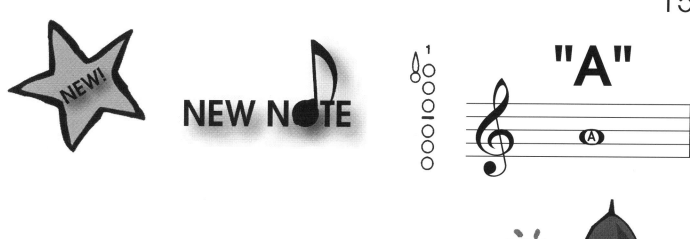

"A"

30. Old MacDonald Had a Farm

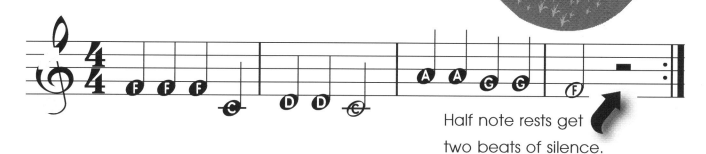

Half note rests get two beats of silence.

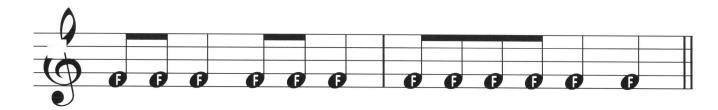

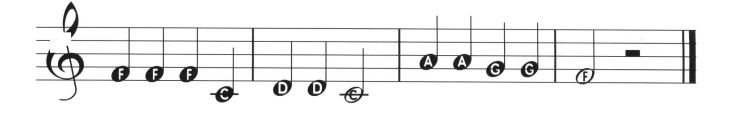

First and Second Endings

When you reach the repeat sign under the first ending, stop and go back to the beginning. When you get to the first ending again, skip it and go to the second ending.

31. Stodola Pumpa

32. London Bridge

Slur

A "slur" is a curved line that connects two or more notes of different pitches. Tongue the first note and move to the next notes without tonguing. Don't stop blowing.

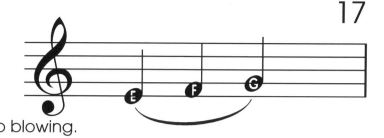

Tie

A "tie" is a curved line that connects two or more notes of the same pitch. Hold the note for the combined value of the notes.

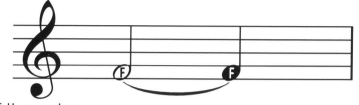

Dotted Half Note

A dotted half note gets three beats of sound.

33. Southern Roses

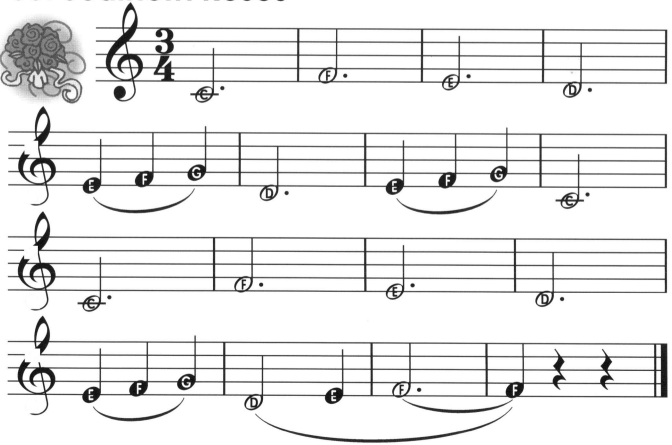

18

Pick-Up Notes

Note(s) that come before the first full measure of a piece of music.

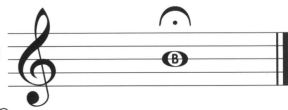

Fermata (Hold)

Hold (keep blowing) the note until your director tells you to stop,

34. Snake Charmer

35. Aura Lee

www.bandfunbook.com

36. Jingle Bells

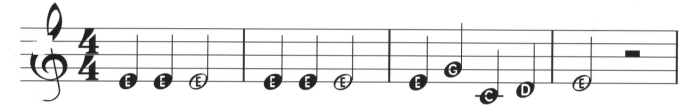

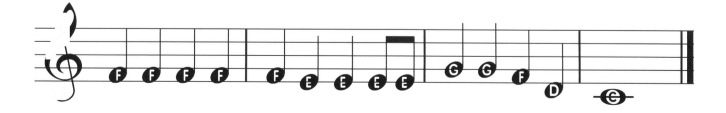

D.C. al Fine

Go back to the beginning
and play until "Fine".

37. Twinkle, Twinkle, Little Star

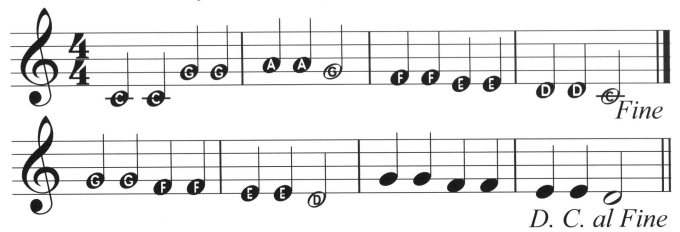

Fine

D. C. al Fine

D.S. al Fine

Go back to the sign and
play until "Fine".

The "sign"

38. Ode to Joy

Fine

D.S. al Fine

Flat Sign

A "flat" lowers the note one half step. It stays in effect for the entire measure.

NEW NOTE "B Flat"

Use your "A" key and your "register" key.

39. Yankee Doodle

Time Signature

A "time signature" tells you how many beats there are in each measure of music.

40. Little Cabin in the Wood

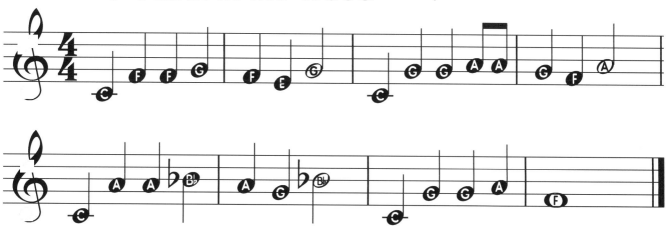

22

Key Signature

A "key signature" changes certain notes throughout a piece of music.

When you see this key signature, play all the B's as B FLATS.

41. It's a Ringer!

 www.bandfunbook.com

42. Polly Wolly Doodle

Sharp Sign

A "sharp" raises the note one half step. It s in effect for the entire measure.

NEW NOTE
"F Sharp"

43. Mary's Other Lamb

44. O Come Little Children (Melody)

45. O Come Little Children (Harmony)

24

46. Jolly Old St. Nick

The Israeli National Anthem, HATIKVA, means "The Hope." Hatkiva expresses the hope of the Jewish people that they would someday return to the land of their forefathers.

47. Hatikvah

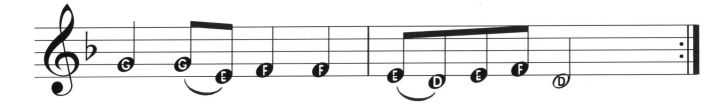

48. Slippery Slurs

Round

Playing the same music beginning at different times.

49. Are You Sleeping?

a Four Part Round

Dynamics

_p_ **Piano**
Play with a soft volume.

_f_ **Forte**
Play with a full volume.

50. Minka, Minka

51. Rollin' Back and Forth

Roll your finger from the first hole up to the "A" key. Don't lift it.

Dotted Quarter Note

A dotted quarter note gets one
and one half counts.

52. America

www.bandfunbook.com

53. Technical Foul

Rhythm Fun

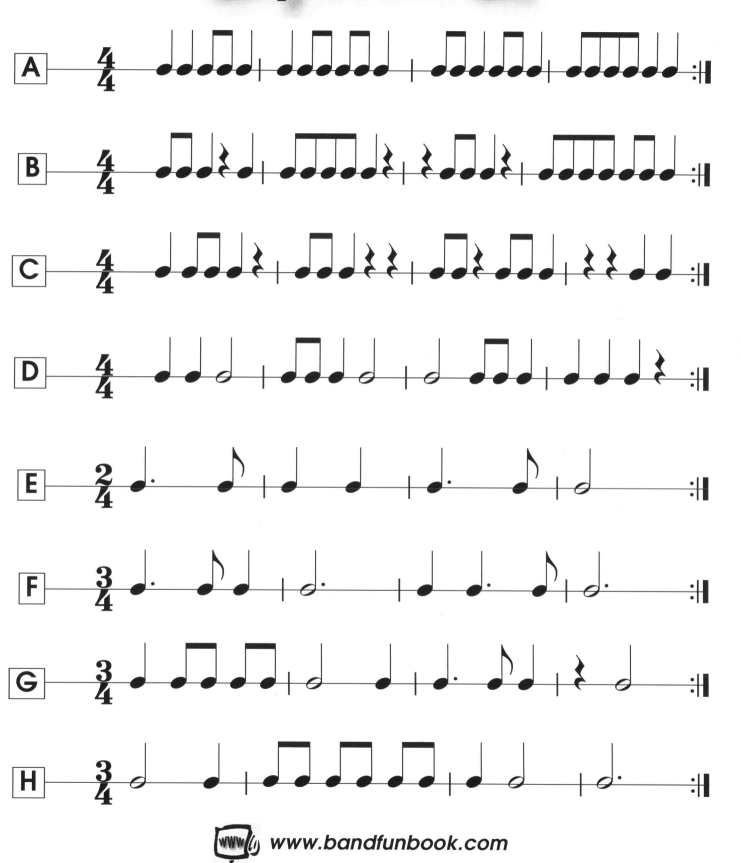

28

54. Rhythm Wreck

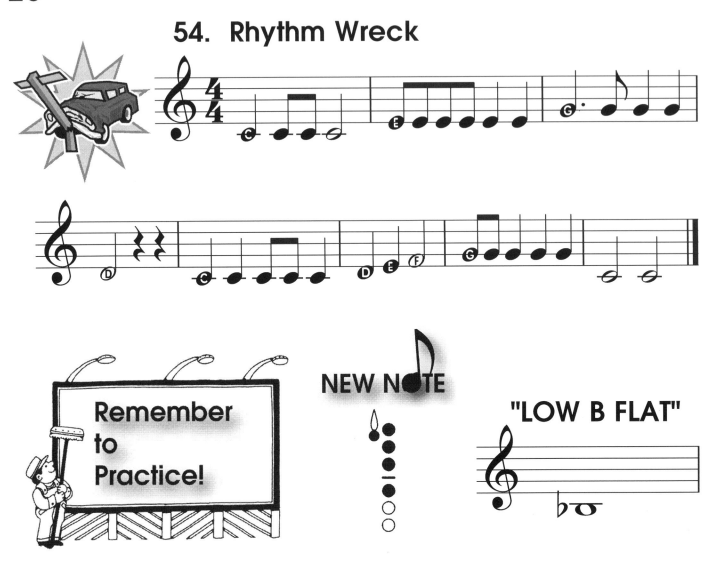

Remember to Practice!

NEW NOTE "LOW B FLAT"

55. More Hot Cross Buns

Natural Sign

A natural sign cancels a flat or a sharp.
It remains in effect for the entire measure.

56. It Just Comes Naturally

57. Don't Be Fooled

 Accent Sign

> An accent sign tells you to play the note with more emphasis.

 Eighth Rest

An eighth rest gets one half beat of silence.

58. Go, Fight, Win!

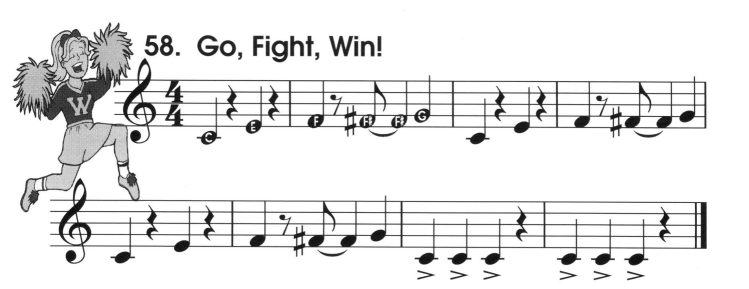

59. Bach Minuet

60. Rueben and Rachel

61. When Love Is Kind

Dynamics

mp **Mezzo Piano**
Play with a medium soft volume.

mf **Mezzo Forte**
Play with a medium loud volume.

62. Mexican Hat Dance

63. Blues Dues

64. Big Breath Slurs

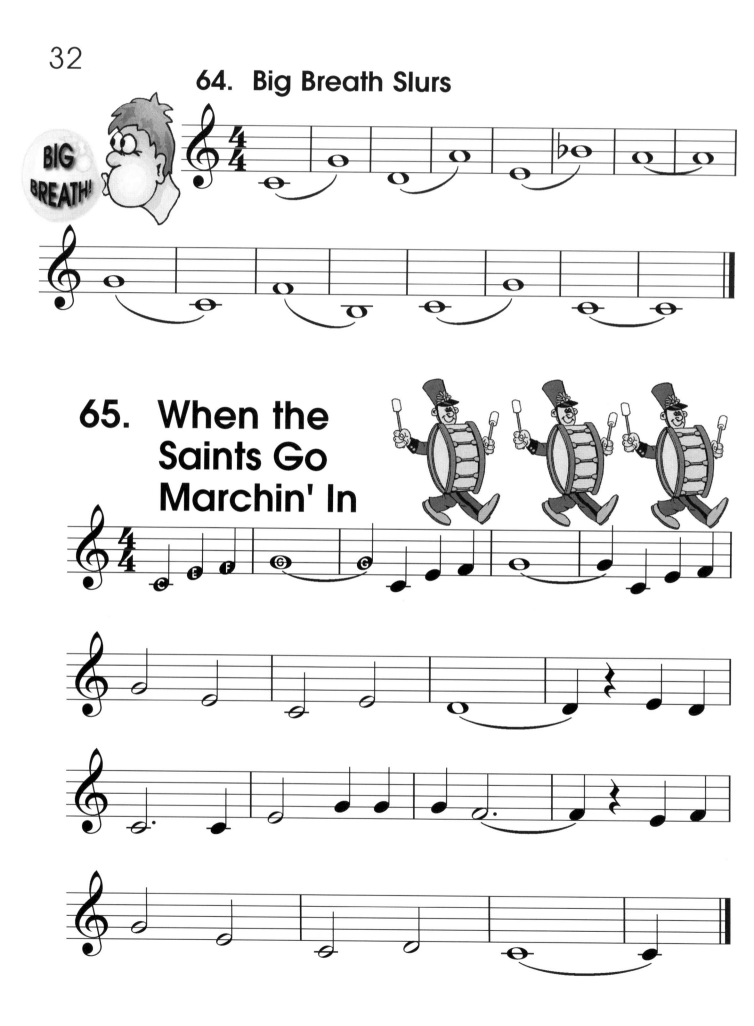

65. When the Saints Go Marchin' In

33

66. William Tell Overture

67. This Old Man

34

NEW NOTE

C SHARP

68. Sweetly Sings the Donkey

69. Danger! Tricky Rhythms

NEW NOTE

LOW A

70. Bye, Baby Bunting

Crescendo *Get louder*

Decrescendo *Get softer*

NEW!

71. Monster Melodies

NEW NOTE

72. Barcarolle

Fun Work

Write in the letters to these notes.

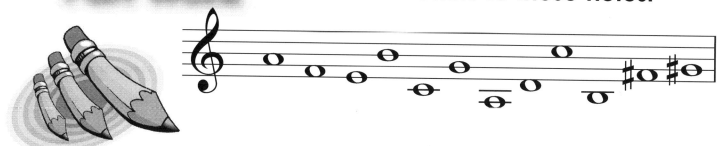

Special Page for CLARINETS

Mary Had A Little Lamb

Stodula Pumpa

London Bridge

Ode to Joy

38

Special Page for **CLARINETS**

Bumpin' UP: G to High D

BUMPIN' UP: F to High C

BUMPIN' UP: E to High B

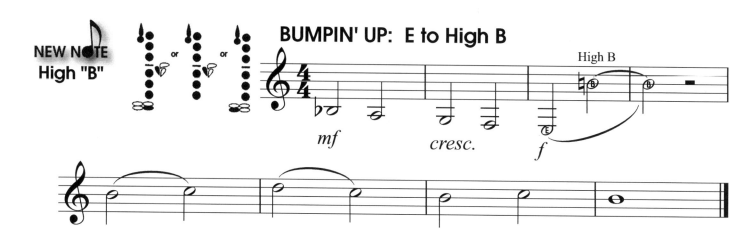

Special Page for CLARINETS

Takin' a Walk to Low G

NEW NOTE
Low "G"

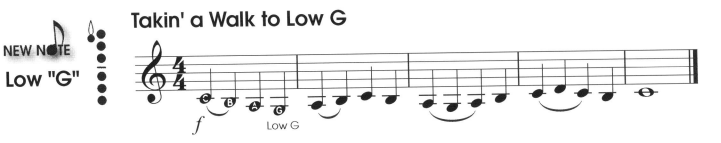

In a Far Off Land

Bumpin' Up: A to High E

NEW NOTE
High "E"

Bumpin' Up: Bb to High F

NEW NOTE
High "F"

Walking Away

Down the Ladder

The Long Ladder

Watch the Slur

Long Slurs

Movin' Faster

Down the Scale

74. Can Can

75. La Bamba

42

76. Simple Gifts

77. Amazing Grace

Bonus Duet Section

The following bonus section features selected beginning duets from **The Beginning Band Fun Book's FUNsembles: Book of Easy Duets for Beginning Band Students**.

This book serves as a great supplement to The Beginning Band Fun Book and contains more than thirty easy and fun to play beginning level duets.

Get your copy online today at **www.bandfunbook.com**

78. Ode to Joy

78. Ode to Joy

79. Italian Song

79. Italian Song

80. Skater's Waltz

81. French Clowns

80. Skater's Waltz

Harmony

81. French Clowns

Harmony

82. Aura Lee

82. Aura Lee

83. Camptown Races

83. Camptown Races

84. Skip to My Lou

Melody

84. Skip to My Lou

Harmony

Clarinet Fingering Chart

● = press the key or cover the hole with your finger.
○ = do not press the key or cover the hole.

When there is more than one fingering given for a note, use the first one unless the alternate fingering is suggested.

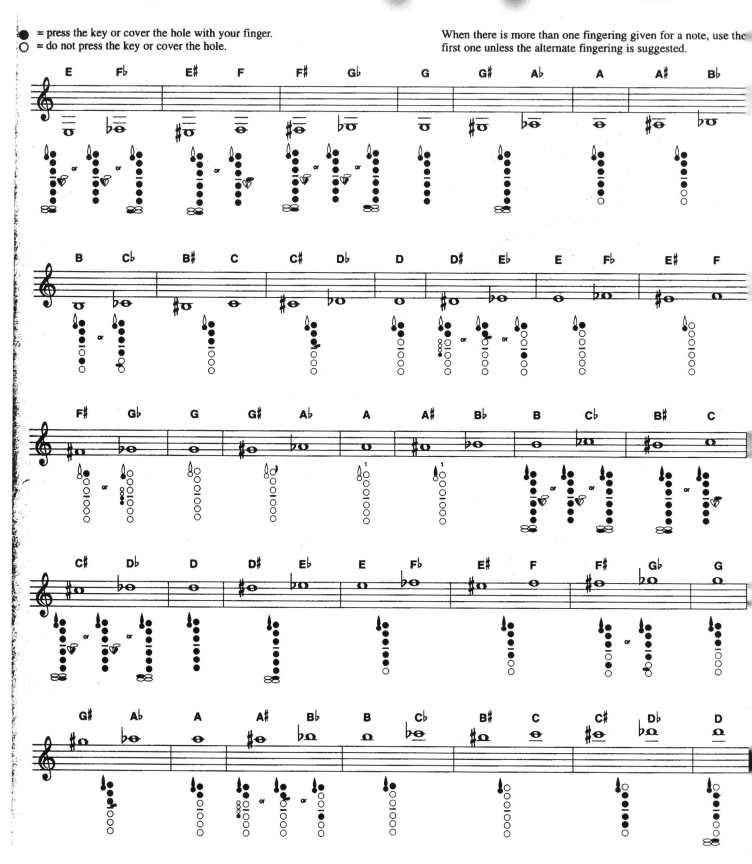